D0093522

Who Is RuPaul?

by Nico Medina

illustrated by Andrew Thomson

Penguin Workshop

To all the legendary children—NM

For Rhia and Cerys—AT

PENGUIN WORKSHOP
An Imprint of Penguin Random House LLC, New York

The publisher does not have any control over and does not assume any responsibility for author or third-party websites or their content.

Visit us online at www.penguinrandomhouse.com.

Library of Congress Cataloging-in-Publication Data is available upon request.

ISBN 9780593222690 (paperback)   10 9 8 7 6 5 4 3 2 1
ISBN 9780593222706 (library binding) 10 9 8 7 6 5 4 3 2 1

Contents

Who Is RuPaul?

On September 18, 2016, RuPaul made television history. (Or "*her*story," as Ru would say.)

A drag queen—most commonly, a man who dresses up and performs as a woman—had never won an Emmy until then. (Emmys are awards for excellence in TV programming, as chosen by the Television Academy.)

Backstage, RuPaul held back tears as he spoke about "all the kids who watch the show." How it had helped them to "navigate their lives."

The show he was talking about was *RuPaul's Drag Race*. Ru is both the host and judge of the reality-competition show of drag queens from across the United States. The queens all share a passion for performing in drag and compete against one another for a cash prize and the title of America's Next Drag Superstar.

According to Ru, drag isn't something unusual to be feared or looked down upon. "Everybody within the sound of my voice is in drag, right now, whether [they] know it or not," RuPaul has said.

What Ru means is, when anyone puts on clothing, they are getting into some form of costume—some type of "drag." When you go to school, you don't put on your bathing suit. Maybe you put on a uniform. You wear what is expected for a student to wear. People dress in "drag" to go to work. To weddings. Out to dinner.

RuPaul says, "We're all born naked and the rest is drag." What Ru means is that we're all the same—and life is a performance.

By the time *RuPaul's Drag Race* won its first Emmy for Outstanding Reality-Competition Program in 2018, 140 drag queens had competed on the show. Many have gone on to have successful careers and thousands of fans of their own.

"We celebrate people who dance outside the box," RuPaul said after the win. Their "stories need to be told, and I think there is value in those stories for everyone, not just drag queens."

RuPaul had traveled a long road to get to that moment. More than thirty-five years before, he had put on his first wig. It had been over twenty-five years since Ru's song "Supermodel (You Better Work)" had hit the airwaves and made him the world's most famous drag queen. And it was nine years since *Drag Race*'s television debut.

But RuPaul had always known he would be famous. Ru has said that to become a star, you need to *believe* you're a star—and eventually, other people will start believing it, too.

As a child in the 1960s, RuPaul hadn't seen many people like him—people who were gay, even people who were Black—on popular TV shows. But things had changed for the better, and Ru had been a part of that change.

"I have always been a creative person," Ru said. "I've always been able to see different colors that other people were ignoring."

How had RuPaul, who came from very humble beginnings, become such a superstar?

This is his—and *her*—story.

He, She, or They? Drag Is for Everyone

RuPaul was once asked if he wished he'd been born a woman. No, Ru answered, he was happy to be a man. (It is a common misunderstanding that drag queens are men who wish to be women.) When RuPaul dresses in drag, he is performing a character. Ru once joked, "You can call me he, you can call me she . . . as long as you call me."

Some drag queens, however, are transgender or nonbinary. For trans people, their gender (how they feel on the inside) is different from the sex (male or female) they were assigned at birth. Nonbinary people do not identify as entirely male or entirely female. These queens might prefer to be called "she" or "they" (rather than "he") when not performing in drag.

Drag *kings* are people—usually women—who dress and perform as men. Women can be drag *queens*, too. Drag is for anyone who wants to express themselves through a character.

CHAPTER 1
"I Accept My Destiny!"

RuPaul's full name is RuPaul Andre Charles. His mother, Ernestine "Toni" Charles, knew this was an unusual name. Before RuPaul was even born, a fortune-teller had told Toni that her son would be famous. So she named him RuPaul because, she said, "ain't another . . . with a name like that."

Toni and RuPaul's father, Irving, were both

from Louisiana. They had met on a blind date. Soon after, they moved to Houston, Texas, and got married. Ru's older twin sisters, Renae and Renetta, were born in 1953.

Irving Charles had served in the army and fought in the Korean War. After the army, Irving moved the family out west to San Diego, California, where he worked as an electrician. The Charles family moved into a three-bedroom house. Irving built a patio out back.

RuPaul was born on November 17, 1960. His younger sister, Rozy, was born two years later.

Renae, Renetta, Rozy, and RuPaul

Ru Stew

According to RuPaul, the *Ru* in his name comes from the word *roux* (say: ROO). Roux is a mixture of flour and butter that is cooked together and used to thicken soups and stews. A roux is used to make gumbo, a hearty Creole dish of sausage, shrimp, other meats, and vegetables.

RuPaul's mother was Creole. Creole people are of mixed descent: Black (African and Caribbean), European (mostly French and Spanish), and sometimes Native American. Creoles have lived in Louisiana since long before it became part of the United States in 1803.

Life in the Charles house was not always easy. RuPaul's parents fought and yelled a lot. When RuPaul was seven, his parents divorced. His mother became so upset that one day, she didn't get out of bed. That's when Ru's older sisters, Renae and Renetta, became the grown-ups in the house. They took care of Ru and Rozy while Toni got the help she needed.

Eventually, Toni got better and found a good, steady job. She worked at a clinic, then later at a local college.

Young RuPaul always knew that he was different from most boys his age. He was quiet and sensitive. He also loved the cigar commercials on television that featured glamorous women, in sparkling evening gowns, performing to Broadway-style music.

When he was four, RuPaul saw something on television that changed his life forever. Diana Ross and the Supremes, a popular musical group at the time, appeared on *The Ed Sullivan Show* and performed their hit song "Baby Love." Ru was captivated.

For one thing, seeing three Black women on a program like Ed Sullivan's was unusual in the early 1960s. And RuPaul saw himself in Diana Ross, the dazzling lead singer, with her perfect hair, beautiful dress, and big, bright

Diana Ross

smile. He remembers thinking: "That one there, the one in the middle—that's me." He knew then that he wanted to be famous—the center of attention—just like Diana.

RuPaul preferred to be around girls rather than boys. He thought that girls and women expressed their emotions and feelings more than boys did. And he liked to play dress-up in their clothes.

"You should have been a girl, and your sister Rozy should have been a boy," some bullies said to him. The hurtful comments sometimes made RuPaul cry.

Still, RuPaul always did what made him happy: He entertained.

Ru's mom and sisters were his first audience. "Do your thing," Toni would tell him, and Ru would stand up, sing, and dance just like the big stars of the day—people like Tina Turner, Cher, and Elvis Presley.

RuPaul looked up to his mom. He loved her simple yet elegant style. And even though Toni could be tough, she also had a sweet and sensitive side. She had "the strength of a man and the heart of a woman."

RuPaul was not afraid to be himself and look different from everybody else. When he was ten, he bleached and braided his hair. At one point, he had a red Afro seventeen inches deep!

RuPaul and Rozy

Ru attended Alonzo E. Horton Elementary School, just a block from his house, from kindergarten through sixth grade. In seventh grade, he took acting lessons at the local children's theater. Ru loved it so much, he signed up for drama at his new middle school.

But aside from drama classes, Ru was not the best student. He often got caught staring out the classroom windows, daydreaming.

RuPaul would rather be home, reading his magazines about Hollywood movie stars, New York City celebrities, and Motown musicians like the Supremes. He loved everything about pop culture: the cool fashion, movies, music, and art that was popular at that time.

Ru sometimes tagged along with his older sisters when they visited their friends Aletha and Deborah. Their mom worked as a maid on the other side of town, so the kids would have the house to themselves in the afternoons. They could listen to records—and sing and dance—as loud as they wanted to!

By the time he entered high school, tall, thin, and freckly RuPaul really stood out from the crowd. With his soft facial features, he was sometimes mistaken for a girl.

In the mornings before class, RuPaul attended Breakfast Club at the cafeteria. Doughnuts, chips, and chocolate milk were served, and the tables and chairs were pushed aside to make room for the students to dance.

RuPaul remembers one morning watching from the sidelines as everyone did a dance called the Bump. Then one day, he and his friend Michelle showed off a move *no one* at Breakfast Club had seen before. It was called the Crypt Walk, the latest dance craze from Los Angeles. (Ru had seen Olivia Newton-John, one of his favorite singer-actresses, perform it on TV.)

Soon everyone was doing the Crypt Walk! That school year, Ru was voted Best Dancer and Best Afro by his ninth-grade classmates. Thinking back on that day, Ru later said that was his way of saying to the universe, "I accept my destiny!" He was born to entertain.

"I accept my destiny!"

What did RuPaul do after introducing the Crypt Walk to his classmates? Well . . . he did *not* go to class. In fact, RuPaul skipped so many classes, he was expelled.

What would he do now? The family decided it was best for Ru to move in with his sister Renetta and her husband, Laurence.

Laurence and Renetta

Laurence was a serious young man with dreams of his own. He was a good role model for RuPaul. He'd earned a scholarship to the University of

California, San Diego, and he dreamed big. Laurence loved to drive around La Jolla (say: la HOY-ah), a wealthy neighborhood on the coast, and look at all the big houses. Sometimes he and Renetta brought her family along.

RuPaul liked Laurence. He was the big brother Ru never had. A father figure, even. But just six months after RuPaul moved in with Renetta and Laurence, the couple decided to move two thousand miles away, to Atlanta, Georgia. There were more opportunities there, Laurence said.

Would Ru like to join them?

"Sure," he said, "why not?"

CHAPTER 2
"RuPaul Is Everything"

In the summer of 1976, fifteen-year-old RuPaul arrived in Atlanta. He enrolled at the Northside School of Performing Arts, eager to start acting again.

Ru's drama teacher, Bill Pannell, taught him

and his classmates about method acting—how to become a character from the inside out. Mr. Pannell was passionate, and even though he expected a lot from his students, he once told RuPaul, "Don't take life too seriously."

Ru said this was some of the best advice he had ever received. Whatever problems he might have, life was a gift to be enjoyed. Other people's problems might be much worse than your own.

One problem RuPaul did *not* have was getting noticed! The funky new kid from California developed a reputation for his bright, bold outfits. Ru used Renetta's sewing machine to make his own clothes.

Stripes? Plaid? A cowboy hat? Why not all three?!

Ru still had problems, however, with school. He continued to skip class, and when he did attend, he was often late. After failing his sophomore year, Ru switched schools. But he never graduated.

RuPaul went to work for Laurence, who had started a business buying luxury cars from around the country and selling them in Atlanta.

After Laurence made a sale over the phone, RuPaul would fly to wherever the car was and drive it back to Atlanta. Ru said he must have driven across the country more than a hundred times. He listened to the radio and sang the whole time.

In 1978, Ru attended his first drag show in Atlanta at a club called Numbers. Drag shows feature drag queens telling jokes, dancing, and performing popular songs, either by singing them or by lip-synching (say: SINK-ing), mouthing the words to a song but not singing them aloud.

RuPaul remembers seeing a drag queen lip-synch a disco hit called "Bad Girls" by Donna Summer. The performance was so good, Ru thought he was watching the real Donna Summer onstage!

RuPaul was hooked. He went back to as many drag shows as he could.

In 1981, RuPaul saw a local TV program called *The American Music Show*. It featured a cast of wacky characters with a weird sense of humor that RuPaul could relate to. Ru wrote a letter to the host, Dick Richards, asking if he could come on the show. Lucky for Ru, Dick said yes!

Dick Richards and RuPaul

House and Ball Culture

The drag queen RuPaul saw that night at Numbers was Crystal LaBeija (say: la-BAY-zhuh), from New York City.

Crystal LaBeija

Like many Black and brown gay teenagers, Crystal had been rejected by her family. So in 1977, she founded the House of LaBeija, opening her home as a place where people like her could live together as their own "chosen" and supportive family. Other drag "houses" followed.

Houses competed as teams against rival houses at drag balls, events that were held mainly in the Black neighborhood of Harlem. Drag balls had taken place in Harlem as early as the 1860s and well into the 1920s, continuing for decades. But the scene grew significantly during the 1980s. The beauty and drama of Harlem's ball and house culture was captured in 1990 by the documentary film *Paris Is Burning* and later in the TV drama *Pose*.

RuPaul says that letter was the true beginning of his career in showbiz.

Before his appearance, RuPaul was helping two girlfriends move into a new apartment. He drove the U-Haul moving truck. Struck by inspiration, Ru told his friends they should start a dance group called RuPaul and the U-Hauls and that they should join him on *The American Music Show*. And so they did!

In January 1982, RuPaul and the U-Hauls made their Atlanta television debut. RuPaul made all their costumes, and they performed a dance routine to the song "Shotgun" by Junior Walker & the All Stars. RuPaul *felt* like a star that day.

Ru and the U-Hauls went on to appear regularly on *The American Music Show*. Dick Richards created a new show called *Dancerama USA* that featured a segment called "Learn a Dance with RuPaul."

RuPaul and the U-Hauls

RuPaul was becoming well-known around the Atlanta music scene. He began performing with other acts. It was at one of these shows that RuPaul dressed in drag for the first time.

A local group called the Now Explosion sometimes acted out a wedding during their performances. At these pretend ceremonies, the boys in the band dressed as bridesmaids, and the girls wore tuxedoes. RuPaul joined them for one of these "weddings."

"It was the first time I did real drag in a dress, heels, and with hair," Ru said. He had never even put on a wig before! "The impact it had on people was amazing."

It made RuPaul *feel* amazing, too. RuPaul wanted everyone to know just how much of a star

he was. So he made posters of himself with phrases like "RuPaul Is Everything" and "RuPaul Is Red Hot." He put up hundreds of copies all over town.

At this time, RuPaul began performing in drag more often. But besides the Now Explosion "wedding," he rarely dressed like a woman in the traditional sense. He wore smeared lipstick, messy wigs, ripped T-shirts, and combat boots—sometimes even tall wading boots like fishermen wore!

"It had nothing to do with being gay" or with "wanting to be a woman," RuPaul said. It was about challenging how people thought about the world. He wanted people to look at things in a different way when they watched him perform.

RuPaul moved into his own apartment. After

RuPaul and the U-Hauls broke up, Ru formed a punk-rock group with two other friends. They performed around Atlanta and up and down the East Coast—they even played in New York City!

RuPaul in New York City

The band broke up in 1984. That year, RuPaul met a local drag queen named Bunny while dancing backup for the Now Explosion. They became fast friends and shopped together at local thrift stores, looking for cheap used clothes to turn into wild outfits.

They didn't want sparkly evening gowns or "any of that polish," Bunny said. They were both rock-and-roll queens. "We . . . broke all the rules," RuPaul said.

Ru continued to host events and put on shows around Atlanta. He sold short books he had written and postcards to anyone who would buy them. Some nights, he sold every copy he had!

Ru, Bunny, and their friends also made campy home movies and sold copies of them around town. (People use the word *camp* to mean something that is done in an exaggerated, theatrical, and often silly style.)

Cher

But RuPaul knew he was destined for bigger things.

He remembered being twelve years old back in San Diego, reading issue after issue of Andy Warhol's *Interview* magazine. Ru had learned that to make it big, he would first have to become a downtown New York celebrity.

CHAPTER 3
Ups and Downs

In the summer of 1984, RuPaul put together a show called *RuPaul Is Red Hot!* Bunny and a few other Atlanta drag queens joined as costars. They traveled to New York City to perform Ru's show at the Pyramid Club in the city's East Village neighborhood.

Andy Warhol (1928–1987)

Andy Warhol once said, "In the future, everyone will be world-famous for fifteen minutes."

Andy was born in Pittsburgh, Pennsylvania. At eight years old, he contracted a rare disease that confined him to his bed for months. During his illness, Andy's mother gave him his first drawing lessons. Andy moved to New York City in 1949, where he worked as a commercial artist for clients like *Glamour* and *Vogue* magazines before focusing on his own artwork.

In 1962, he painted one of his most famous works, *Campbell's Soup Cans*. This was the beginning of the "pop" ("popular") art movement, which turned everyday elements of people's lives—things like Coke bottles and hamburgers—into art. Warhol also painted a series of celebrity portraits in the same bold, bright style, including one of the actress Marilyn Monroe. He quickly became a celebrity himself, and his art studio—called the Factory—became a popular hangout for artists, musicians, and fashionable New Yorkers. In 1969, he founded *Interview* magazine, which publishes new issues to this day.

After the run of shows ended, Ru and his friends decided to stay in New York. They met an old friend of Dick Richards's from back in Atlanta named Nelson, who showed them around the city. Nelson introduced them to the work of the creative queer people who had come before them—like playwright Tennessee Williams and author Truman Capote.

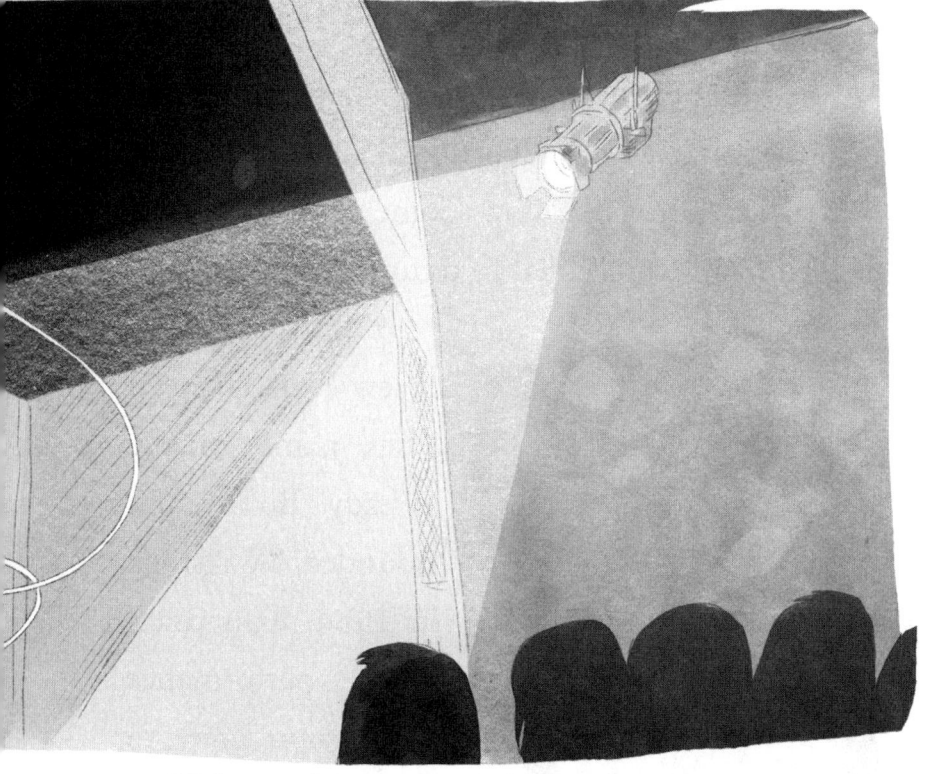

Nelson always carried a video camera, and RuPaul was always happy to put on a performance. In one video, RuPaul tells the camera, "I'm gonna take off like a stick of dynamite."

But life in New York wasn't easy. Ru and Bunny made forty dollars a night dancing at the Pyramid Club, but Ru didn't have a place to live. Some nights, he stayed with Nelson or other friends.

Other nights, he and Floydd—another friend from Atlanta—would stay out all night, then sleep in parks during the day. Come Christmastime, Floydd and Ru decided to return home.

Bunny stayed in New York, changed her name to the "Lady" Bunny, and founded Wigstock in 1984. This drag-queen performance festival soon grew to attract thousands of people every year.

In 1985, RuPaul began to rethink his act in Atlanta. Dick Richards offered him a record deal. Ru starred in local theater productions and more than a dozen movies. He sold video cassettes of the films out of shopping carts at local bars and clubs.

One of Ru's movie characters, a fashion model who was also an undercover spy named Starrbooty, starred in three movies. Ru, with his massive Mohawk and creative, self-designed looks, gave each performance his signature, over-the-top best. And it was always in his contract that RuPaul's name appeared above the movie title. After all, he was the star!

Ru also worked at a local gay bar called Weekends. When the bar owners reopened the old movie theater next door, RuPaul began to emcee, or host, drag pageants and lip-synching competitions there. He watched videos of himself onstage to improve his skills as an entertainer. Ru called his time at Weekends his "college years."

By 1987, Ru had really made a name for himself in Atlanta. But he was growing restless.

It was time to give New York another try.

That summer, he and a couple of friends—DJ Larry Tee and another Atlanta drag queen called Lahoma—piled into a van to make the journey. On the drive, one of the back tires blew out, and the van flipped over. Their belongings scattered across the highway.

No one was hurt, but this felt like a sign of things to come.

Finding success in New York City was no easier the second time around for RuPaul. By the spring of 1988, he was back in Atlanta. Although Ru returned to New York again that summer, things were just not happening the way he had hoped.

Ru tried his luck in Los Angeles next, moving in with his younger sister, Rozy. But he couldn't find work, and Rozy gave him until November 17, his twenty-eighth birthday, to find a new place to live. It was a dark and difficult time. Ru went to San Diego to spend the holidays with his mother. But where would he go from there?

First, he rested. He quit smoking and grew a beard. He spent time getting to know his eleven-year-old niece Morgan. He ate well, and he relaxed.

Ru also talked on the phone with DJ Larry Tee who, after more than a year in New York, had found success in the nightclub scene. Larry told

RuPaul that he was a star and that Ru should come back. He offered to help Ru out when he arrived.

So in the new year, RuPaul returned to New York City yet again.

But this time would be different.

Larry Tee

CHAPTER 4
Queen of Manhattan

In the New York nightclub scene in 1989, the trendy "look" for drag queens was "realness." That meant that queens looked less camp and more like "real" women.

So RuPaul reinvented himself.

He traded in his Mohawk for a big blond wig. He shaved his legs. And no more ripped T-shirts and wading boots. When RuPaul walked into a club, he wanted to be the most glamorous, gorgeous woman in the room!

The late 1980s and early 1990s marked the era of the Club Kids. The Club Kids were party promoters whose job was to bring crowds into nightclubs. Before going out on the town, the Club Kids would dress up in outrageous, imaginative, and attention-grabbing looks. They used their creativity to turn these parties into must-see events that no one wanted to miss.

"A Club Kid was a little crazier than a drag queen," Lady Bunny said. They might "dress up as an alien or a dog bowl . . . from the waist up, and a policeman from the waist down."

But Club Kids were about more than dressing up. RuPaul said they were about "people being free spirits." Club Kid culture would go on to inspire the drag, art, and fashion worlds for years beyond the 1990s.

While RuPaul didn't dress like the Club Kids, he became just as well-known in New York City nightclubs. At seven feet tall in heels and hair, he was hard to miss!

Susanne Bartsch

Susanne Bartsch—who became "the Mother of all Club Kids" and continues to throw parties today— hired Ru to dance at some of her legendary events.

RuPaul gave it his all, every single time. He didn't just dance—he *performed*! RuPaul was a show all by himself.

Susanne clearly respected Ru's talent. She told him that he had what it took to become a true pop star.

The summer after Ru returned to New York, Larry Tee started throwing a new party called the Love Machine. Larry paid RuPaul a hundred dollars a week to host shows, lip-synch, and dance there.

"Everybody say love!" Ru would call out to the partygoers.

"Love!" everyone would shout back.

Lady Bunny, Floydd, and Lahoma—all of Ru's Atlanta friends—made the Love Machine their home base. Their easy Southern charm took New York by storm, and the Love Machine quickly became the hottest party in town.

Tools of the Trade

A drag queen's character is typically an exaggerated, campy image of how women look. To create this illusion, drag queens have some tricks up their sleeves:

Makeup—Drag queens paint their faces "for the back row," meaning someone watching a drag show from the back of the crowd can still see a drag queen's expressive face in great detail.

Hair—Sometimes, one wig is not enough! Queens sometimes "stack" multiple wigs together to create a big, attention-grabbing shape.

Corset—Tight-fitting garment that goes above the hips and under the chest, to give the illusion of a small waist.

Padding—Gives a drag queen wider hips.

Around this time, the B-52's—a pop-music group from back home in Georgia—asked RuPaul to appear in a music video for their hit song "Love Shack." Ru showed up to the video shoot in an all-white two-piece jumpsuit, bright gold jewelry, and a large Afro wig. He brought his dance-party energy to the set!

By January 1990, a year after moving back to New York, RuPaul was becoming very well-known. A group of downtown club owners and party promoters named him "Queen of Manhattan." This was a big deal in the New York nightlife community, and Ru was the first Black person to earn the title.

At last, RuPaul had arrived!

But with success came pressure. RuPaul was living a fast-paced life, and for years, he had turned to drugs and alcohol during his long, party-filled nights.

So as his reign as Queen of Manhattan came to a close at the end of 1990, RuPaul decided to quit his bad habits—and reinvent himself once again.

CHAPTER 5
Supermodel of the World

In 1991, RuPaul joined World of Wonder, a production company founded by Randy Barbato and Fenton Bailey. Randy and Fenton had met RuPaul in New York in the early 1980s and had produced his *Starrbooty* album. Now they became Ru's managers. Soon, Ru had a contract with Tommy Boy Records.

RuPaul got busy writing new music. He was also promoting "I Got That Feeling," a new song he and Larry Tee had written the year before. But when Ru performed "Feeling" for audiences, he didn't appear in his signature, glamorous drag-queen look.

RuPaul didn't think the world beyond the New York City club scene was ready for a drag queen to be a pop star. But people kept asking what had happened to his Starrbooty character. RuPaul began to realize that fans really wanted to see him perform in drag.

Ru had never imagined he would become famous by performing in drag, but he decided to go all out. If this was what his fans wanted, he would give them "the longest legs, the highest shoes," and "the biggest hair" he could!

He would give them a Supermodel of the World.

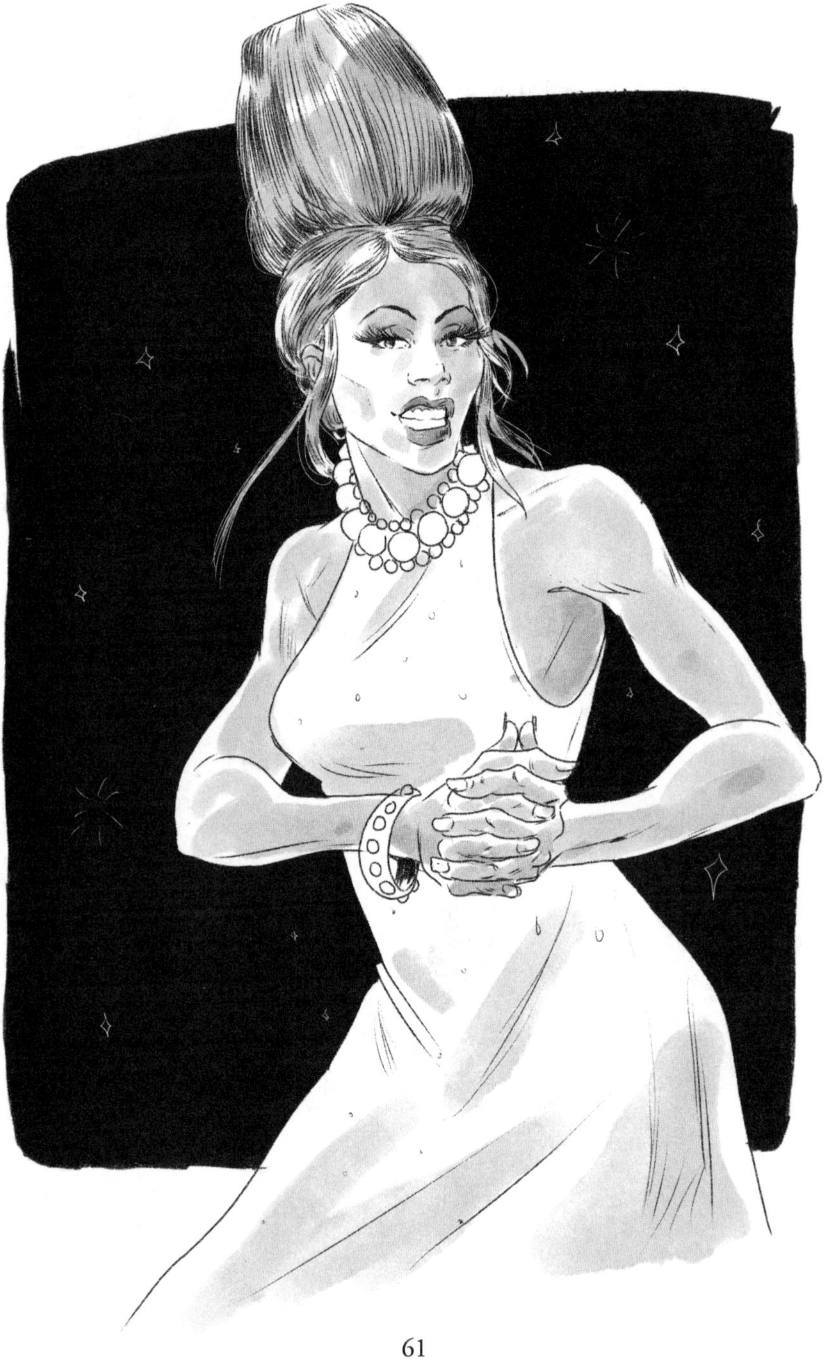

In the early 1990s, fashion models like Naomi Campbell, Linda Evangelista, Claudia Schiffer, and Christy Turlington were major international celebrities. These "supermodels" posed in exotic

locations around the world for stylish fashion shoots. They earned large salaries and were photographed wherever they went.

RuPaul's newest song, "Supermodel (You Better Work)," captured the excitement of the moment. Ru premiered it with a live performance at Lady Bunny's Wigstock festival on Labor Day 1992. The single was released on Ru's birthay in November of that year. A full album, *Supermodel of the World*, followed in 1993.

In the "Supermodel" music video, RuPaul plays a model on a photo shoot in New York City. She strikes poses for the camera. She splashes around in a fountain in front of the famous Plaza Hotel. She struts down the sidewalk with a group of schoolgirls like they are walking a fashion-show runway.

Perhaps remembering his drama teacher Mr. Pannell's advice, RuPaul also had fun in the video, not taking herself *too* seriously. As she lip-synched

to the catchy lyrics, she made silly, exaggerated faces for the camera.

"Supermodel" became a hit, reaching number two on the dance charts. MTV, a cable network that showed music videos, aired the video over and over again. Most people around the country had never seen a drag queen before, in person *or* on television. But there was RuPaul, front and center: seven feet of legs, heels, hair, and attitude.

RuPaul appeared on *The Arsenio Hall Show*,

a popular late-night talk show. Backstage, he was nervous. But then Ru remembered all the years of practice he'd had performing for the camera, entertaining audiences, and making people feel good.

After performing "Supermodel," Ru sat down to chat with Arsenio and the studio audience. Ru had everyone laughing, but he also delivered a serious, heartfelt message. "Everybody is really

the same," RuPaul said. "Everybody wants to be loved" and "should be respected." That love, he said, started with loving yourself.

Ru said he was lucky his family accepted him for who he was, because there were many other gay people—children and adults—who couldn't say the same. He hoped that by appearing on a program like Arsenio's, he might inspire people watching at home, the same way that seeing a young Black woman like Diana Ross on *The Ed Sullivan Show* had inspired him.

"Everybody say love!" he called to the crowd.

"Love!" they responded.

America was only just meeting RuPaul, but RuPaul had worked his whole life for this moment. He was no newcomer. From rowdy Atlanta bars to smoky New York City nightclubs, he had put in the time and effort.

Just like Ru's song says, if you want to be a superstar: "You better *work*."

A Brief History of Drag

Dressing in the traditional clothing of the opposite sex—called cross-dressing—has existed throughout history. Ancient civilizations from the Egyptians to the Aztecs incorporated cross-dressing into religious ceremonies. During William Shakespeare's time, women's roles onstage were played by men. The word *drag* may have originated in the 1800s theater scene because the men's dresses would "drag" on the floor. In the early 1900s, female impersonation—men performing as women—became popularized in live vaudeville acts, which combined music, dance, and comedy. Female impersonation by non-queer men continued in movies like *Some Like It Hot* (1959) and *Mrs. Doubtfire* (1993). Drag became more closely connected with gay culture during Prohibition in the 1920s, when liquor was outlawed in the United

States, and queer people—including drag queens—met in secret, illegal bars called speakeasies. Drag continued to evolve in local gay bars, before going nationwide in 1972 with the first Miss Gay America pageant.

Men in drag in the late 1800s

CHAPTER 6
"Windows of Opportunity"

In Atlanta, RuPaul Was Everything. At the Pyramid Club, RuPaul Was Red Hot. And now . . . RuPaul Was *Everywhere*!

The song "Supermodel" played at New York Fashion Week runway shows. It was used in a commercial for Duracell batteries. RuPaul performed it at the Cannes Film Festival in France. He presented at the MTV Video Music Awards. And Ru's yearlong concert tour played to packed crowds across the United States and Europe.

A few years earlier, after RuPaul had moved back in with his mom in San Diego, Toni told her son, "Everything will change, so pay it no mind." She sure was right. What a difference five years had made!

The world had changed a lot in that time, too. Queer people everywhere—people who were gay, lesbian, bisexual, and transgender—were "coming out of the closet." They were declaring to friends, family, and the world who they truly were and

who they loved. And they were demanding to be treated equally.

On April 25, 1993, as many as one million people joined the March on Washington for Lesbian, Gay, and Bi Equal Rights and Liberation. They had come to the nation's capital to protest laws that discriminated against queer people. And they called on Bill Clinton, the newly elected president, to fulfill his promises to the queer community and to fight on their behalf.

When Drag Was a Crime

"Masquerade laws," which banned people from dressing in costumes, or in the clothing of the opposite sex, spread across the United States during the mid to late 1800s. Throughout the 1940s, '50s, and '60s, these laws were used by police to arrest many gay people.

There were also laws against people of the same sex dancing together.

Bars where gay people and drag queens gathered to dance were often raided by the police. When the Stonewall Inn—a bar in New York City's Greenwich Village neighborhood—was raided in the early-morning hours of June 28, 1969, the people inside fought back . . . and won. What followed was a nationwide movement for queer rights that continues to this day.

RuPaul took the stage in a red-white-and-blue Wonder Woman–inspired look. As "Supermodel" blasted from the speakers, a cloud of dust rose as thousands rushed toward the stage.

He couldn't believe where he was, gazing toward the Washington Monument, the National Mall stretched out before him.

There Ru was, standing in the same spot where Dr. Martin Luther King Jr. gave his famous "I Have a Dream" speech in 1963. RuPaul realized he now had a responsibility to the queer community. His days of running wild from club to club were over. Still, never one to take things too seriously, after the song ended, RuPaul told the crowd that he'd be back one day . . . to paint the White House pink!

After his performance, Ru received a terrible phone call. His mother had passed away. Toni had been ill for a while, and Ru had known this day was coming. Still, he was heartbroken. Toni had been one of his original inspirations, his first true fan, and the person who always believed in him. And now she was gone.

But RuPaul carried on.

The March on Washington, 1963

The civil rights movement of the 1950s and '60s saw African Americans fighting—through peaceful protest—for equal rights and protection under the law. Across the South, Jim Crow laws had separated the races—from hotels and restaurants to train cars and drinking fountains. And people had had enough.

Those who opposed equal rights for Black Americans often responded violently, injuring and sometimes killing the activists who were calling for change. With new laws stalled in the United States Congress, the March on Washington for Jobs and Freedom was organized by Dr. Martin Luther King Jr. and other leaders to demand that these laws be passed. The demonstration took place on August 28, 1963, on the National Mall in Washington, DC. More than 250,000 people attended.

In 1994, Ru met his future husband, Georges LeBar, at the Limelight nightclub in New York City. Georges was "dancing like a maniac" when RuPaul approached him and asked if he could put his arms around him. Georges is six feet eight inches tall, and Ru was not used to people being taller than he was! (And Georges said yes.)

"Throughout history there are . . . windows of opportunity," Ru once said. During the early 1990s, "there was an openness happening" in America. And RuPaul took full advantage.

Ru became the first drag queen to be named spokesperson for a major makeup line, MAC's VIVA GLAM. He published a book about his life called *Lettin It All Hang Out*. He hosted a morning radio talk show with Michelle Visage, an old Club Kid friend.

In 1994, Ru made his feature-film debut in Spike Lee's *Crooklyn*, followed by *The Brady Bunch Movie* and TV shows like *Sister, Sister*. In 1995, he appeared in *To Wong Foo, Thanks for Everything! Julie Newmar*. The movie featured

John Leguizamo, Patrick Swayze, and Wesley Snipes—male lead actors known for their roles in comedy, romance, and action movies—all playing drag queens. Drag culture had come to Hollywood!

Wesley Snipes, Patrick Swayze, and John Leguizamo in *To Wong Foo*

But not all the attention Ru received was positive. Tabloid newspapers published untrue stories about him. Their headlines poked fun at him. He became the butt of jokes on popular TV and radio shows. But RuPaul always took comfort in the advice Toni had given him when he was teased in school: "Unless they're paying your bills, pay them no mind."

From 1996 to 1998, RuPaul (along with his cohost Michelle Visage) hosted one hundred episodes of *The RuPaul Show* on the cable channel VH1. He was the first openly gay man—and certainly the first drag queen—to host a talk show. *The RuPaul Show* featured big-name guests like the Backstreet Boys and *NSYNC, as well as Ru's childhood idols Olivia Newton-John, Cher, and—of course—Diana Ross.

How much higher could RuPaul's star rise?

CHAPTER 7
"Start Your Engines!"

RuPaul moved to Los Angeles in 1998 and continued releasing music into the early 2000s. But while new songs like "Looking Good, Feeling Gorgeous" were played on dance radio stations and in nightclubs, nothing reached the same level of success as "Supermodel."

Ru took time away from the spotlight to recharge. Despite his glamorous public personality, RuPaul was really a quiet, shy person at heart. Ru went on hikes and hosted barbecues. He spent time with Georges, friends, and family.

Ru's longtime friends and collaborators at World of Wonder—Fenton Bailey and Randy Barbato—were wondering what would come next

for RuPaul. They had lots of ideas, but nothing seemed right. Fenton remembers Ru once telling him, "I'll do anything but a competition and elimination show."

But by 2008, Ru had changed his mind. In the fifteen years since "Supermodel," no other drag queen had risen to RuPaul's level of fame. It was time to bring drag culture back into the mainstream—out of big-city nightclubs and into people's living rooms.

And so . . . *RuPaul's Drag Race* was born!

Drag racing is a race between two cars to see which driver crosses the finish line first. Courses are straight roads called "drag strips" and are usually about one quarter of a mile long. Naming the show "Drag Race" was a fun way to use a term people were familiar with for something that had never been seen on TV before.

According to Ru, *Drag Race* was a way to "celebrate the art of drag" and to "put a face and an emotion" behind it. RuPaul had already told the world his story. But there were thousands of other, lesser-known drag queens across the country who had their own voices and stories to tell. Ru wanted to give them the opportunity to inspire young people to be themselves and follow their dreams.

The first season of *RuPaul's Drag Race* premiered in February 2009 on Logo—a cable TV channel that aired mostly queer content. The show featured nine drag queens competing to win a prize package that included being named America's Next Drag Superstar.

RuPaul has described the show as a mix between *Project Runway* and *America's Next Top Model*, two popular competition shows for hopeful fashion designers and models. To win the title, America's Next Drag Superstar needed to show they had the most *charisma* (personality), *uniqueness* (originality), *nerve* (bravery), and *talent*.

Each episode starts with a "mini challenge"— a fashion photo shoot, for example—as well as a "maxi challenge." On episode one, "Drag on a Dime," RuPaul challenged the queens to create looks out of materials from a discount "dollar store."

Episode One: "Drag on a Dime"

As host, RuPaul plays double duty. He appears dressed in men's clothes to lay out the rules of the challenges, then later to check on the queens' progress in the workroom. Ru asks the queens questions about their lives and what inspires them. And he gives them advice for how to perform well in the maxi challenge.

After the challenges, the queens must walk the runway on the Main Stage in their best drag. RuPaul hosts this portion of the show in drag. Having taken inspiration from actual supermodel Tyra Banks, the original host of *America's Next Top Model*, RuPaul plays every bit the tough critic, letting the contestants know exactly what she liked—or didn't like—about their looks and performances.

Next, RuPaul discusses with her panel of judges, which since 2011 has featured her longtime friend Michelle Visage. Ru listens to everyone's thoughts on who were the strongest and weakest queens of the week. But ultimately, the choice is RuPaul's.

After Ru names the winner of the episode, she announces the bottom two drag queens (those with the lowest scores). These queens must lip-synch to a song of Ru's choosing. Ru, the judges, and the other contestants are then treated to a dramatic drag performance.

Finally, Ru must decide whom to eliminate.

Borrowing lyrics from the song that made her famous, RuPaul tells the winner of the lip sync, "Shanté, you stay." And to the loser: "Sashay away."

RuPaul carries his message of love to *Drag Race*, too. At the end of every episode, RuPaul tells the contestants, "Now remember: If you can't love yourself, how . . . you gonna love somebody else? Can I get an 'Amen!' up in here?"

Amen.

Other challenges on *RuPaul's Drag Race* have included the queens writing rap verses to songs, learning dance numbers, performing stand-up comedy, filming TV commercials, and hosting their own talk shows—many of the things RuPaul himself had done over the years. Before they can even *think* about winning the crown, RuPaul's queens needed to *work*!

BeBe Zahara Benet, the first winner of *RuPaul's Drag Race*

Not many people tuned into *RuPaul's Drag Race* in 2009. But with each new season, the show gained more fans. In 2016, *Drag Race* won an Emmy award, the first of many more to come. For its ninth season, in 2017, *Drag Race* moved from Logo to VH1, and its viewership doubled. Now it is regularly the most popular cable show in its time slot. In 2019—across cable, streaming, and online—the show was watched more than 190 million times!

Bob the Drag Queen

Over thirteen seasons (and counting) and more than 170 episodes of the show so far, fans have met drag queens from all corners of the country and from many walks of life.

Hilarious queens like Bianca Del Rio and Bob the Drag Queen. High-fashion queens like Raja and Aquaria. Accomplished dancers like Alyssa Edwards and Shangela. Kooky queens like Jinkx Monsoon, and queens who sometimes dressed more like monsters than glamorous women, like Sharon Needles and Yvie Oddly.

Shangela

"[These queens] are teaching young people how to . . . find their light and to shine in that light," RuPaul said.

As the show's popularity skyrocketed, more famous celebrities appeared on the show as guest judges—stars like Lady Gaga, Miley Cyrus, Christina Aguilera, Nicki Minaj, Neil Patrick Harris, and Adam Rippon, to name a few.

And if you think RuPaul's star couldn't shine any brighter . . . hunty, she is just getting started.

Lady Gaga and RuPaul

Drag Slang

Over the years, many of the catchphrases used by the queens of *RuPaul's Drag Race* have made their way into mainstream culture. While these sayings did not begin with *Drag Race*, the show has helped popularize some of them beyond the queer community.

Hunty or *henny*—another way to call someone "honey"

Yas and *werk* (or *werq*)—different ways to say and spell "yes" and "work"

Sickening—when something is so good, it makes you sick!

Slay—to perform very well; to kill (slay) the competition

Reading—to insult another queen but in a clever and playful way

What's the T or *tea?*—the "T" stands for "truth";
to "spill tea" is to speak the truth

Kiki—to gossip, to spill tea

CHAPTER 8
"Werk" the World

RuPaul and his award-winning TV show have taken the world by storm.

Ru continues to record new music and regularly features his songs, like "Cover Girl" and "Sissy That Walk," on the *Drag Race* Main Stage. He

has published new books—*Workin It!* (2010) and *GuRu* (2018)—and has appeared in TV shows like *The Simpsons* and *Ugly Betty*. He also stars in his own scripted Netflix series, *AJ and the Queen*.

RuPaul's Drag Race has also spawned spin-off shows, all of which RuPaul hosts and works on as an executive producer. On *Drag U,* women who feel like they've lost their sense of glamour and confidence are given "drag makeovers" and life lessons by drag-queen "professors." On

RuPaul's Secret Celebrity Drag Race, famous men—and women—are put into drag by queens from the show. There have also been multiple seasons of *RuPaul's Drag Race All Stars,* a series in which queens who performed well on their seasons return to compete for a spot in the *Drag Race* Hall of Fame.

The *Drag Race* phenomenon has also gone global, with international versions of the show airing in the United Kingdom, Thailand, Chile, and Canada. *Drag Race* queens have teamed up and toured the world together. In 2020, a number of fan-favorite queens—including Naomi Smalls and Asia O'Hara—starred in a live stage show that ran for more than a month at the Flamingo Las Vegas Hotel and Casino.

In 2015, the first RuPaul's DragCon, a convention for all things drag, drag queens, and *Drag Race*, took place in Los Angeles. It expanded in 2018 to New York City, and in 2020 to London, England. Thousands of fans go to these conventions every year.

At DragCon, fans can buy anything they need for a fabulous drag look, attend panel discussions, meet queens from the show, and watch drag performances. Some DragCon attendees come in drag themselves!

Many of the fans are teenagers or younger. "Parents come up to me . . . and say [the show] helped them understand their queer child a little bit more," Michelle Visage said. "This little TV show has changed and saved so many people's lives."

"That's the revolution right there," RuPaul said of these young fans. "They are our hope for the future."

In 2018, RuPaul was honored with a star on the Hollywood Walk of Fame. Jane Fonda, one of Ru's childhood idols, presented him with the honor. But she said the star "should be at least three sizes bigger" because no one "else has ever launched an industry like RuPaul has. . . . Behind the glamour," she said, ". . . is a man of great depth, incredible intelligence, and compassion."

People around the world have embraced RuPaul's message of self-love and respect. They have been inspired to express their creativity through the art of drag . . . and to pay their naysayers no mind.

"*Everybody* say love!"

Timeline of RuPaul's Life

1960	RuPaul Andre Charles is born on November 17 in San Diego, California
1976	Moves to Atlanta and enrolls at Northside School of Performing Arts
1978	Attends first drag show
1982	Makes his television debut on *The American Music Show*
1984	Presents his showcase, *RuPaul Is Red Hot!*, at the Pyramid Club in New York City
1986	Starrbooty character is born in Atlanta
1989	Stars in the B-52's music video for "Love Shack"
1990	Named "Queen of Manhattan"
1993	"Supermodel (You Better Work)" music video debuts
1994	Meets future husband, Georges LeBar
1995	Releases autobiography *Lettin It All Hang Out*
1996	Begins hosting daily talk show, *The RuPaul Show,* on VH1
2009	*RuPaul's Drag Race* premieres on Logo
2015	RuPaul's DragCon opens in Los Angeles
2016	Wins his first Emmy Award
2017	Marries longtime partner, Georges LeBar
2018	Presented with a star on the Hollywood Walk of Fame
2020	RuPaul's DragCon opens in London

Timeline of the World

1961	Communist East Germany begins building the Berlin Wall to separate East and West Berlin
1969	Uprising at the Stonewall Inn, a gay bar in New York City, inspires a nationwide movement for LGBTQ+ rights
1970	First annual gay-pride marches held across the United States to honor the anniversary of Stonewall
1981	MTV (Music Television) cable channel is launched
1982	Madonna releases "Everybody," her first single and video
1984	Michael Jordan plays his first NBA game
1989	Berlin Wall begins to be torn down
1993	President Bill Clinton signs Don't Ask, Don't Tell into law, which allowed queer people to serve in the military, if they kept their identities a secret
1997	After more than 150 years under British rule, Hong Kong becomes part of China
2001	The Netherlands becomes the first country in the world to legalize same-sex marriage
2010	President Barack Obama repeals Don't Ask, Don't Tell
2015	Same-sex marriage is legalized across the United States
2018	In Sweden, Greta Thunberg begins a school strike to protest her government's response to climate change
2020	NBA superstar Kobe Bryant dies in a helicopter crash

Bibliography

Braithwaite, Les Fabian. "2017: RuPaul Is Everything." *Out*,
   25th anniversary issue, October 2017.

Lawson, Richard. "The Philosopher Queen." *Vanity Fair*, Holiday
   2019/2020. Print.

"RuPaul Biography.com." **Biography.com**. Last modified April 16,
   2019. https://www.biography.com/personality/rupaul.

RuPaul. *Lettin It All Hang Out: An Autobiography*. New York:
   Hyperion, 1995.

Snetiker, Marc. "The Oral History of RuPaul." **Time Inc.**, 2020.
   https://ew.com/tv/2017/06/15/rupaul-first-lady-of-drag-
   lgbtq-issue/.